# Real Food FOR Dogs

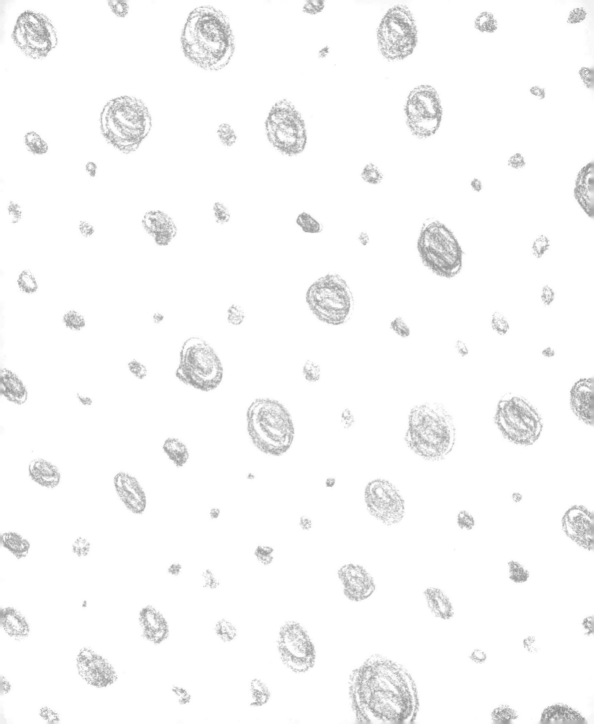

# Real Food FOR Dogs

## 50 Vet-Approved Recipes to Please the Canine Gastronome

**by Arden Moore**
**Illustrated by Anne Davis**

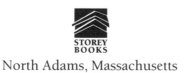

STOREY
BOOKS

North Adams, Massachusetts

*The mission of Storey Publishing is to serve our customers by publishing practical information that encourages personal independence in harmony with the environment.*

Edited by Nancy W. Ringer and Larry Shea
Cover design and art direction by Meredith Maker
All illustrations © Anne Davis
Text design by Kathy Herlihy-Paoli
Text production by Jennifer Jepson Smith
Indexed by Nan Badgett/word•a•bil•i•ty
Many thanks to Veterinary Nutritional Consultations
   for reviewing the manuscript and recipes

Printed in the United States by R.R. Donnelley
10  9  8  7  6  5  4  3  2  1

**Library of Congress Cataloging-in-Publication Data**

Moore, Arden
   Real food for dogs: 50 vet-approved recipes to please the canine gastronome / by Arden Moore.
      p. cm.
   Includes bibliographical references and index.
   ISBN 1-58017-424-8 (alk. paper)
   1. Dogs—Food—Recipes. I. Title.

SF427.4 .M66 2001
636.7'0855—dc21                                          2001049086

# DEDICATION

To Sassy, Cosmo, and Foxi and dogs everywhere
that deserve flavor-filled home-cooked meals made with love.


# ACKNOWLEDGMENTS

I wish to thank all the veterinarians, nutritionists, and dog owners who generously shared their expertise and recipes to make this book a canine cuisine delight. Special thanks to Rebecca Remillard, D.V.M., Ph.D., Lowell Ackerman, D.V.M., Mark W. Jackson, D.V.M., Ph.D., and my editor, Nancy Ringer.

# CONTENTS

## VEGETARIAN MEALS ..................... 61

Mollie's Marvelous Veggie Casserole ▪ Doggy Vittles
No-Meat Stew ▪ Paws-Up Potato Casserole
Lip-Smacking Green Beans ▪ Tempting Tofu ▪ Mac Attack
Si, Si Tortillas ▪ Pooch Pancakes ▪ Spinach Surprise

## SPECIAL OCCASION MEALS .............. 81

Munchy Pup-cakes ▪ Fido Thanksgiving Feast
Beans and Bacon Stir-Fry ▪ "Go Fetch" Stew
Birthday Breakfast Bonanza

## SPECIAL DIETS ................................. 97

Puppy Growth Diet ▪ Meal for Active Dogs
Meal for Senior Dogs ▪ Doggie Diet for Inactive Canines
Hypoallergenic Diet

# INTRODUCTION

I remember the day my Dad came back from the grocery store, placed a brown bag full of food on the kitchen counter, and announced: "This is for Crackers."

Crackers was our family's rotund beagle that my Dad affectionately nicknamed "Pickle Barrel." Our veterinarian told us that she was extremely overweight and needed to be put on a pound-trimming diet.

Effective immediately, Dad ordered, we were no longer to succumb to Crackers's begging brown eyes by sneaking her portions of our meals: strips of bacon, bits of hamburgers, and ice cream cones. We became Crackers's personal chefs, preparing healthy, low-calorie meals of steamed brown rice, vegetables, lean ground beef, and boiled chicken.

Preparing "people food" for our family dog seemed strange at first, but then we saw the results: a happier, healthier — and slimmer — Crackers who shed the "Pickle Barrel" nickname and who lived to be 16.

Yes, folks, food is fuel — for people AND for dogs. The right "fuel" keeps our dogs fit and frisky. Our dogs are full-fledged members of our families and deserve to be served nutritious, well-balanced meals.

We are fortunate that dog food has become quite a popular subject to study. Veterinary nutritionists working for major commercial dog food companies have created a whole array of foods specific to a dog's age, health, activity level, and yes, even breed.

Yet your dog deserves a variety, a periodic break from the same old chow found in his bowl. *Real Food for Dogs* contains 50 veterinarian-approved recipes sure to get your dog drooling with delight — and begging for seconds (but resist, resist).

The beauty of this book is that the recipes are easy to make, easy to keep as leftovers, and often edible for you, too! Now, I'm not saying that you'd give up a piece of carrot cake to snack on Great Gravy Cookies, but you may find Chow Hound Chicken Soup or Canine Casserole doggone delicious. I know I do.

Prepare these recipes once a week or for special occasions as a tasty substitute for a commercial dog food that contains a necessary balance of nutrients. You'll improve your relationship with your dog, hone your cooking skills (why not try out a new recipe on your chow hound?), and save some money on the weekly food bill. As for your dog, you may find him at mealtimes with his tail happily tapping the kitchen floor, and a napkin tucked into his collar.

Bone appetit!

# TREATS

**ogs seem to be lousy spellers** until you spell the word t-r-e-a-t. Before you can finish the final "t," most are making a hairpin turn around the kitchen chair and heading full throttle to you as you hold that tasty, homemade delight. Admit it — shouting the word "treat" also fills you with happiness as you watch your pooch light up with anticipation.

So, don your apron, warm up the oven, and bring out the mixing bowls. It's time for you to step into the role of doggie chef and your dog to become your treat taster!

# PARMESAN PLEASER

For the dog that loves Italian seasoning, here is a flavorful treat that will reap tail-wagging encores for more. Viva la cheesy cookies!

2 cups whole wheat flour
⅓ cup vegetable oil
⅓ cup powdered milk
1 egg
¼ cup Parmesan cheese
2 teaspoons garlic powder

1. Preheat the oven to 350°F.

2. In a blender or a food processor, thoroughly blend all ingredients. Add just enough water to form a stiff dough consistency.

3. Use a wooden rolling pin dusted with flour to roll out the dough to ½-inch thickness.

4. Place the dough on an ungreased cookie sheet.

5. Bake for 15 to 20 minutes.

6. If you want crunchy treats, turn off the oven and let the cookies stay in the oven for an additional hour. For more doughy treats, remove the tray right away.

7. Allow the giant treat cookie to cool before breaking it into small pieces.

8. Store the pieces inside resealable plastic bags in the refrigerator.

# THE DOGGIE CHEF'S TEN COMMANDMENTS

As you venture into the taste-filled world of homemade meals for your dog, please keep these ten tips in mind:

1. Wash your hands in warm soapy water and rinse well before handling food.
2. Clean all produce in cold water to wash away any pesticides, dirt, and bugs.
3. Trim meats of fat, and drain excess grease from cooked meats.
4. Keep the recipe simple.
5. Select fresh and, if possible, organically grown ingredients.
6. Opt for variety.
7. Always cook meat, seafood, poultry, and eggs.
8. Provide fresh, filtered water daily.
9. Serve two or three small meals daily, not one large one.
10. Store leftovers in airtight containers in the refrigerator, where they will keep for up to four days, or in the freezer, where they will keep indefinitely.

# LEAP FOR LIVER

Foxi, a plump Pomeranian, prefers to perch on the couch most of the day. But she perks up and starts yipping and prancing when her owner, Karen Cichocki of Dyer, Indiana, brings out the liver from the refrigerator and the food processor. That tandem means only one thing: Liver treats are soon on their way!

"Foxi loves these liver treats as much as my husband, Rick, loves my chocolate chip cookies," notes Cichocki. "I make enough in a batch to freeze some and hand them out as treats for Foxi."

    1  pound sliced beef liver (save the juice)
    ¼  cup water
    1  small box corn muffin mix

1. Preheat the oven to 350°F.

2. In a food processor, blend the liver one slice at a time on high until liquefied. Add a little water as you add each slice.

3. Pour the corn muffin mix into a large bowl. Then add the liver liquid and mix thoroughly.

4. Spray an 8½- by 11-inch baking pan with nonstick spray.

5. Pour the liver mix into the pan.

6. Bake for 20 to 25 minutes, or until the middle springs back at your touch.

7. Cool and cut into small cubes. Store the cubes in resealable plastic bags in the freezer.

# BOW-WOW BROWNiES

Dogs give a paws-up to this tasty treat. It offers the sweetness of chocolate but in the safer form for dogs: carob. Make a batch and cut them into bite-size pieces to use as rewards for well-behaved performances.

½ cup vegetable oil
2 tablespoons honey
1 cup whole wheat flour
4 eggs
1 teaspoon vanilla
½ cup carob chips
¼ cup carob powder
½ teaspoon baking powder

1. Preheat the oven to 350°F.

2. In a medium-sized bowl, blend the oil and honey thoroughly using a wooden spoon.

3. Add the remaining ingredients and mix well.

4. Pour onto a greased 15- by 10-inch baking sheet.

5. Bake for 30 to 35 minutes.

6. Let cool, then frost (see recipe at right) if desired.

7. Cut into bite-size squares and store in a sealed container in the refrigerator.

# BOW-WOW BROWNIE FROSTING

12 ounces fat-free cream cheese
1 teaspoon honey
1 teaspoon vanilla

1. In a small mixer, blend all three ingredients.

2. Use a spatula to spread the frosting over the pan of cooled brownies.

## OBESITY DANGERS

Your dog isn't opening up the refrigerator on his own and helping himself to midnight snacks. Often the culprit behind a dog's chubbiness is his owner. An overweight dog weighs between 20 to 25 percent above the ideal weight for his particular breed and age. An obese dog weighs 30 percent or more above the ideal weight for his breed and age.

A combination of too much food (especially table scraps) and too little exercise can lead to a dog developing severe chronic conditions such as diabetes, heart problems, arthritis, muscular injuries, and respiratory problems.

# DOG BISCUITS BAKED WITH LOVE

♡♡♡♡♡

Mmmmm . . . here is one of my favorite treat recipes that is sure to win over your dog.

      2  cups unbleached wheat flour
      1  cup cornmeal
      Pinch of salt
      1  egg
      3  tablespoons vegetable oil
      2  teaspoons chopped fresh parsley
      ¾  cup chicken broth

1. Preheat the oven to 400°F.

2. Mix the flour, cornmeal, and salt in one bowl.

3. In a separate and larger bowl, whip the egg with the oil, parsley, and chicken broth. Add the flour mixture and mix until a soft dough forms.

4. Knead the dough and roll it out to ½-inch thickness. Use cookie cutters to cut the dough into canine-pleasing shapes, such as cats, cars, and fire hydrants.

5. Bake for 15 minutes. Cool the biscuits before serving.

# GREAT GRAVY COOKIES
♡♡♡♡♡

Your meat-loving dog will "Sit" on command if you serve this easy-to-make recipe. Hey, where is it written that cookies must be sweet to taste good?

2½ cups whole wheat flour
2 small jars beef-flavored baby food
6 tablespoons beef gravy
1 egg
½ cup nonfat dry milk
½ cup water
1 tablespoon brown sugar
½ teaspoon garlic powder
½ teaspoon salt

1. Preheat the oven to 350°F.

2. Combine all ingredients in a large mixing bowl.

3. Lightly pat your hands with flour and shape the mix into a big ball.

4. Flatten the ball using a floured wooden rolling pin.

5. Use a cookie cutter to cut the dough into triangles or stars. Place the cookies on a greased cookie sheet.

6. Bake for 25 minutes, or until lightly browned.

7. Allow the cookies to cool before serving.

## CAUTION: FOOD DANGERS AHEAD

Some foods, like onions, can be tolerated by different dogs to different degrees, from a fair amount to not at all. With other foods, like chocolate, you should not feed even a morsel to your dog, no matter how he begs for a bite of that tasty-looking candy bar. Here are some foods to watch out for in your dog's diet, from limit to completely omit.

### Mind the Milk

A few occasional laps of milk from your cereal bowl may be okay, but don't serve your dog milk at every meal. Some dogs lack lactase, the enzyme needed to break down the lactose (milk sugar) in milk, and may suffer from diarrhea if they ingest milk.

### Oust the Onions

In small quantities, onions may be relatively safe for dogs, but why take the chance? The constituents of onions can trigger diarrhea, vomiting, and fever. In addition, onions contain large amounts of sulfur, which can destroy red blood cells and cause severe anemic reactions in dogs.

### Beware of Real Bones

Even though dogs love to chew bones, and chewing helps to reduce tartar build-up on their teeth, bones can cause many problems for dogs, such as vomiting, diarrhea, constipation, intestinal obstructions, and internal bleeding. Opt for a safer alternative to those big soup bones: rawhide chew strips or nylon bones.

### Resist Raw Meat

Raw meat carries the threat of bacteria and parasites. Of particular concern are salmonella, a bacterial organism that can cause a variety of diseases in both animals and people, and certain species of tapeworm that can be found in raw meat and passed on to a pet that ingests the meat.

### Steer Clear of Sushi

You may love an occasional dinner of raw tuna or salmon sushi rolls, but skip any notions of serving your dog sushi. Raw fish, especially smelt, herring, catfish, and carp, contains an enzyme called thiaminase, which destroys the vitamin thiamine ($B_1$). Fortunately, cooking destroys this enzyme.

### Cut Out the Chocolate

Chocolate can be downright deadly to your dog. It contains theobromine, a dangerous chemical that can cause severe, life-threatening diarrhea in dogs. Baking chocolate is especially harmful to dogs because it contains nearly nine times more theobromine than milk chocolate does. As little as 3 ounces of baking chocolate can kill a 25-pound dog. If you want to make a sweet treat for your dog, substitute carob for chocolate.

# SAY CHEESE, PLEASE

No need for a camera to get your dog to strike a pose while trying to earn a few of these cheese pleasers.

   1½  cups water
    1  cup quick-cooking oats, uncooked
    ¼  cup margarine, softened at room
       temperature
    1  cup grated cheddar cheese
    1  egg, whisked
    ½  cup powdered milk
   Pinch of salt
    1  cup cornmeal
    1  cup wheat germ
    3  cups whole wheat flour

1. Preheat the oven to 325˚F.

2. Bring the water to a boil.

3. Pour the hot water into a large bowl and add the oats and margarine.

4. Stir the mixture and let stand for 5 minutes.

5. Add the cheese, egg, milk, and salt and stir with a spoon.

6. Blend in the cornmeal and the wheat germ.

7. Slowly add the flour, ⅓ cup at a time, until you form a stiff dough.

8. Roll out the dough to ½ inch thickness.

9. Cut into dog- or bone-shaped biscuits with cookie cutters.

10. Place the biscuits on a baking sheet coated with nonstick spray.

11. Bake for 50 minutes, or until the biscuits are golden brown.

12. Turn off the heat and let the biscuits remain inside the oven for 1 hour to make them crunchy.

13. Allow to cool and serve as treats or homemade kibble.

# SIX NECESSARY NUTRIENTS

All dogs, from the Shih Tzu to the Saint Bernard, depend on these six classes of nutrients for growth, maintenance, and repair of tissues:

- Carbohydrates
- Fats
- Protein
- Vitamins
- Minerals
- Water

Carbohydrates, fats, and protein provide the major ingredients to build tissue and produce energy in the body. Vitamins, minerals, and water perform other roles such as maintaining a healthy red blood cell supply, keeping bones strong and dense, and keeping tissues hydrated and body temperatures regulated.

# CHICKEN DIPPED TREATS

Okay, so maybe the notion of combining a chicken bouillon cube with powdered milk in the SAME recipe doesn't tempt your taste buds, but just test this recipe on your dog.

1¾ cups water
1 cup quick-cooking oats, uncooked
⅓ cup margarine, softened to room temperature
1 chicken-flavored bouillon cube
¾ cup powdered milk
1 egg, whisked
¾ cup cornmeal
3 cups whole wheat flour

1. Preheat the oven to 325°F.

2. Bring the water to a boil.

3. Pour the water into a large bowl and add the oats, margarine, and bouillon cube. Mix well and let stand for 5 minutes.

4. Stir in the powdered milk, egg, and cornmeal.

5. Slowly add the flour, ½ cup at a time, mixing with a wooden spoon.

6. Knead the dough a few minutes to create a stiff consistency.

7. Using a rolling pin, roll out the dough until it is ½-inch thick.

8. Cut the dough into golf ball–size circles and place on a greased cookie pan about 1 inch apart.

9. Bake for 45 to 50 minutes, or until the treats are golden brown.

10. Remove the pan from the oven. Let the treats cool until hard and crunchy.

# CANINE COOKIES

\* \* \* \*

Keep a steady supply of these cookies on hand for your canine chum.

    2  cups quick-cooking oats
    4  chicken bouillon cubes
    ½  cup margarine
    2  cups boiling water
    2  cups whole wheat flour
  1½  cups yellow cornmeal
    1  cup nonfat milk
    2  eggs
    2  tablespoons sugar
    2  cups grated cheddar cheese
       All-purpose flour

1. Preheat the oven to 350°F.

2. Spray cookie sheets with nonstick cooking spray.

3. Mix together the oats, bouillon cubes, and margarine in a large bowl.

4. Add the boiling water and allow the heat to dissolve the bouillon cubes and margarine.

5. Add the remaining ingredients except the all-purpose flour.

6. Form the mix into a big ball, adding flour as needed to make a stiff dough.

7. Roll out the dough to ½-inch thickness. Use dog- or bone-shaped cookie cutters to cut out cookie shapes. Place them on the cookie sheets.

8. Bake for 10 to 12 minutes, or until golden brown.

9. Let the cookies cool completely before offering as treats.

# DOGGIE DELIGHTS

Serve up this meal to add shine to your dog's coat and a lively step to his walk.

2 cups whole wheat flour
½ cup rice flour
½ cup soy flour
¼ cup powdered milk
1 tablespoon chopped fresh parsley
1 teaspoon garlic powder
1 package active dry yeast
¼ cup warm water
1 cup chicken stock
1 egg
1 tablespoon skim milk

1. Preheat the oven to 350°F.

2. In a large bowl, combine the flours, powdered milk, parsley, and garlic powder.

3. In a small bowl, dissolve the yeast in the warm water.

4. Add the chicken stock to the yeast.

5. Combine the liquid mixture into the large bowl and knead for 3 to 4 minutes.

6. Sprinkle a cutting board with flour. Use a wooden pin to roll out the dough on the cutting board to a ¼-inch thickness.

7. Cut out dough into bone shapes; place them on an ungreased cookie sheet.

8. Beat the egg with the skim milk. Brush the dough lightly with this glaze.

9. Bake for 45 minutes. Turn off the heat and let the biscuits dry an additional 2 hours inside the oven.

10. Cool before serving.

# MUST-HAVE MUFFINS

Here's a sweet sensation filled with wholesome goodness.

    1½  cups oat flour
     1  cup oat bran
     1  cup rolled oats
     2  teaspoons cinnamon
     2  teaspoons baking soda
     1  egg, whisked
    ⅓  cup honey
     3  tablespoons sunflower oil
    ¾  cup skim or nonfat milk

1. Preheat the oven to 425°F. Spray a 12-muffin pan with nonstick spray.

2. In a large bowl, mix the flour, bran, oats, cinnamon, and baking soda.

3. In a separate bowl, blend the egg, honey, and oil.

4. Add the milk to the bowl with the dry ingredients and then add the egg, honey, and oil mix. Stir well.

5. Spoon into the muffin pan, filling the cups three-quarters full.

6. Bake for 15 to 20 minutes.

7. Cool before serving. Store extras in resealable plastic bags in the freezer.

## BALANCING ACT

Feeding your dog tail-wagging treats is certainly lots of fun for him (and for you), but
making sure his diet provides good all-
around nutrition is even more
important. Here are some things
to keep in mind.

### The Fabulous Five

Dogs, just like us, benefit from eating
items from the five main food groups:

- Breads and cereals and other
  grain products
- Vegetables
- Fruits
- Meats and fish
- Milk, cheese, and dairy products

### Pass the Peas, Please

Make sure that your homemade meals include a good portion
of non-meat foods, especially grains, vegetables, and starches.
Some excellent non-meat foods that are highly nutritious and tasty
to canines are rice, bagels, oatmeal, green beans, tortillas, peas,
broccoli, and spinach.

# FRUITY PUP-SICLES

Curb your dog's drive to chew on inappropriate objects — namely, your favorite dress shoes — by offering one of these fruit-filled chills. This icy treat will keep your dog occupied for a long time — and save your shoes!

- 1 quart orange juice
- 1 banana, mashed
- ½ cup plain yogurt

1. Mix all the ingredients in a container with a spout. Pour the blend into empty ice cube trays.

2. Store in the freezer until you want to serve up a treat.

23

# MEATY MEALS

**Dogs are born meat lovers.** They crave protein and often try to charm you with their baby browns into giving them second helpings. Resist, resist. You want your dog to be fit and healthy.

Here are some fun main dish recipes to make. My personal favorite is Canine Casserole, but your dog may howl in delight when you fill his bowl with Marvelous Mutt Meatballs. The best news: Some of these recipes are also pleasing to people's palates. So, schedule a time for you and your dog to enjoy a dinner date together. And, pass the mutt meatballs, please!

# CANINE CASSEROLE

In my quest to perfect this recipe, I found five very willing canine taste testers at the Seal Beach Animal Care Center in Seal Beach, California. They gave this dish a very positive seal of approval. Rudy, a Labrador-Akita mix, couldn't wait a second longer and actually leaped on top of the serving table before I could put the food bowl down on the ground. Laura, a German shepherd mix with a touch of arthritis, and Roscoe, a Labrador–Pit Bull mix, demonstrated the best manners by slowly but methodically licking their bowls clean. Chinook, a Husky with one brown and one blue eye, won the speed contest, inhaling a full bowl within 33 seconds, while Reeka, an Australian Cattle Dog mix, proved to be the most picky — she strategically nosed out all the carrots and gulped down the rest of the casserole.

I wish to thank these five delightful dogs and all the volunteers at the Seal Beach shelter for the opportunity to "test market" this casserole.

2 cups brown rice, uncooked
½ pound ground chuck hamburger
1 teaspoon vegetable oil
1 garlic clove, crushed
½ cup finely chopped carrots
½ cup finely chopped broccoli

1. Cook the rice in a steamer.

2. Steam the carrots and broccoli until tender.

3. Warm the vegetable oil in a pan over medium heat. Add the hamburger and garlic and sauté until cooked through.

4. Combine all the ingredients.

5. Allow to cool before serving. Store leftovers in the refrigerator.

# TiME-SAViNG TiPS

Preparing a homemade meal for your dog may take less time than you realize. Here are some ways to whip up meals in minutes:

- Set aside an hour on Sundays and make a large recipe that can be divided into two or three meals during the week. Or make two recipes at a time and freeze one of them.

- Rely on your microwave to steam vegetables and reheat doggie leftovers in a hurry.

- Make once-a-week meals that both you and your dog can enjoy. (A couple of suggestions — the recipes for Marvelous Mutt Meatballs on page 33 and for No-Meat Stew on page 65.)

- Let stews and other dishes simmer all day in a Crock-Pot.

## THE TRUTH ABOUT CARNIVORES

Contrary to popular belief, canines are not carnivores (strictly meat eaters). They are omnivores, animals that feed on both animal and plant substances. True, your dog's great-great-great-granddad may have hunted prey in the prairie, but remember, the prey he ate (such as rabbits and birds) were herbivores that ate only plants. In eating the rabbit, he also ate the plants the rabbit had eaten. Your dog's digestion system is engineered to digest and absorb protein from plant sources as well as from meat.

# BIG DOG DELIGHT

For dogs with hearty appetites — or, if you want to make enough chow to last a week — try this recipe. Your dog will say Woof!

>     2 medium yams
>     3 cups cooked brown rice (natural, unprocessed)
>  1½ pounds beef liver (or chicken liver)
>  1½ pounds pork shoulder blade steak (fat and bone removed)

1. Preheat the oven to 350°F.

2. Wash and dry the yams. Using a fork, stab each yam twice to produce two series of holes. Place in the oven and bake for 40 minutes, or until a fork can easily slide through the yam.

3. In a skillet, brown the liver on both sides. Cook until done but not overly done. It's okay if the center is a little pink. Set aside.

4. Place a little oil in a frying pan and brown the pork shoulder blade steak on both sides. Cook until done. The center should not have any hint of pink.

5. In a food processor, combine all ingredients in three batches, using two parts meat to one part yam and one part rice. Blend until the mix has achieved a putty consistency.

6. Pat the mixture into hamburger-size patties — about 3 or 4 tablespoons per patty.

7. Place patties in resealable plastic bags or storage containers.

8. Freeze portions intended for consumption later in the week. Store servings for today and tomorrow in the refrigerator.

## A Trip to the Dog Food Aisle

Most days you probably just don't have the time to prepare a delicious home-cooked meal for your pup. But when you are in the supermarket, strolling past those endless cans and packages with pictures of happy dogs, it's a good idea to know a little more about the food you're going to buy for your buddy.

### Finding the Right Type for Fido

For you history buffs, here's a little bit of trivia. The first commercial dog foods were introduced in the United States in the late 1890s. Back then, dogs ate baked biscuits made with a blend of meat, vegetables, and grains — no kibble.

Today, commercial dog foods come in these main forms:

• **Dry.** In general, dry dog foods contain 35 to 50 percent carbohydrates, 18 to 27 percent protein, 7 to 15 percent fat, and less than 12 percent moisture. The hard pieces of kibble help prevent major buildup of tartar and plaque on dogs' teeth.

• **Semimoist.** This form offers an irresistible taste and texture and typically contains 25 to 35 percent carbohydrates, 16 to 25 percent protein, 5 to 10 percent fat, and about 30 percent water.

• **Canned.** Obviously the all-time favorite among most canines, canned food costs the most per serving but delivers the highest palatability. Brands vary, but most canned foods contain 8 to 15 percent protein, 2 to 15 percent fat, and about 75 percent moisture.

### Deciphering Dog Food Labels

As required by guidelines estab-
lished by the Association of American
Feed Control Officials, a quality commercial dog food product should contain
the following:
• Guaranteed analysis of nutrients
(percentage breakdown of crude protein, fat, fiber,
and moisture)
• Ingredient listing in descending order of predomi-
nance by weight
• Additives listing
• Net weight
• Manufacturer contact information, including a toll-free
consumer information number
• Nutritional adequacy statement indicating if this product
provides complete and balanced nutrition for all dogs or for a
particular life stage
• Feeding directions that offer general guidelines
• Caloric statement

### Meat, Cereal, and . . . What's This?

Just like in people food, additives are used in commercial
pet foods to enhance the quality, flavor, and appearance of the
food and to preserve freshness. The most commonly used additives include antioxidants (to keep fat from becoming rancid),
anti-microbial agents (to slow down spoilage), colors (to improve
appearance), and emulsifiers (to prevent water and fat from
separating).

# BABY, OH BABY

**H**ere's a yummy meal that you can make in mere minutes.

> 3  small jars beef or chicken baby food
> ½  cup Cream of Wheat

1. In a glass bowl, mix the baby food and Cream of Wheat with a spoon.

2. Cover the bowl with a lid and place inside the microwave. Set it to high for 3 to 4 minutes.

3. Cool before spooning out.

# MARVELOUS MUTT MEATBALLS

Have some fun and hone your dog's fetching skills by tossing him a few of these meatballs at dinnertime.

½ pound ground beef
⅓ cup grated cheddar cheese
1 carrot, finely chopped
½ cup bread crumbs
1 egg, whisked
1 teaspoon garlic powder
1 teaspoon tomato paste

1. Preheat the oven to 350°F.

2. Combine all ingredients in a medium-sized bowl.

3. Scoop out by the spoonful and roll into mini-size meatballs.

4. Place the meatballs on a cookie sheet sprayed with nonfat cooking spray.

5. Bake for 15 to 20 minutes.

6. Cool and store in the refrigerator in a container with a lid.

# GOBBLE DOWN GOULASH

This odd collection of ingredients may cause your nose to turn up, but it's pure delight for your dog.

2 raw carrots, shredded
½ cup green beans
1 cup cabbage
1 pound ground beef
2 tablespoons olive oil
2 eggs
1 14-ounce can of baked beans
1 tin sardines
1 garlic clove, crushed

1. In a blender or food processor, purée the carrots, green beans, and cabbage.

2. Brown the ground beef with the olive oil in a large saucepan. Stir in the egg.

3. Add the vegetables, baked beans, sardines, and garlic to the beef.

4. Simmer over low heat, covered, for 20 to 25 minutes, stirring occasionally.

5. Cool before serving.

# HOWLING GOOD STEW

Your dog will bay at the moon for second helpings of this dish.

>     4  ounces ground beef
>     2  cups cooked brown rice
>     1  hard-boiled egg, mashed
>     2  slices white bread
>     1  teaspoon calcium
>        carbonate

1. Brown the ground beef in a pan over medium heat.

2. In a large bowl, mash together the cooked beef, the rice, the egg, crumbled pieces of bread, and the calcium carbonate. Stir well.

3. Cool before serving.

37

# TLC LEFTOVERS

Time to clean out the fridge? Your dog will drool for this medley of goodies left over in your refrigerator.

> 4 ounces lean ground beef
> 4 ounces low-fat or fat-free cottage cheese
> 1 cup grated or cooked carrots
> 1 cup cooked and chopped green beans
> 1 teaspoon bonemeal powder

1. Cook the ground beef in a pan over medium heat. Drain off the fat. Allow meat to cool.

2. Add the remaining ingredients and mix well.

## DOGGIE DIETS

Veterinary nutritionists say dogs placed on "crash diets" run the risk of losing more muscle mass than excess fat. If your dog needs to go on a weight-reduction diet, work with your veterinarian to formulate a diet plan that gradually cuts back on on your dog's daily calories. Ideally, a dog that is 30 percent overweight should take about six months to reach an ideal weight through reduced portions. This slow but steady plan melts off the pounds — and keeps them off.

# BACON-BEGGING MEAL

There is something about bacon — maybe the smell, maybe the taste — that is absolutely irresistable to a dog. This is a highly popular meal among my canine taste testers.

- 2 pounds beef liver
- 2 slices bacon, cooked
- 2 cups bread crumbs
- 2 garlic cloves, minced
- 2 eggs, slightly whisked
- 2 teaspoons vegetable oil
- 2 tablespoons whole wheat flour
- 1 cup water

1. Preheat the oven to 350°F. Spray a loaf pan with nonstick spray.

2. Put the liver in a large bowl and pour boiling water over it. Let sit about 10 minutes, then drain.

3. Place the liver in a food processor and blend until it is a thick paste.

4. Add the bacon, bread crumbs, garlic, and eggs, and mix thoroughly.

5. Press this mix into the loaf pan.

6. Bake for 45 to 50 minutes, or until the top has browned.

7. Warm the oil in a small saucepan over low heat. Stir in the flour to form a paste.

8. Slowly pour in the cold water and simmer over low heat for about 5 minutes, until the gravy thickens. Stir often.

9. Pour the gravy over the liver loaf, allow to cool, and then serve.

10. Store the leftovers in the refrigerator or freezer.

smells fantastic

# MMMMM MEAT LOAF

▽△▽△▽△▽

Here's a hearty meal that both you and your dog can devour.

>  2  slices whole wheat bread
>  2  pounds lean ground beef
>  ½  cup milk
>  1  egg
>  1  teaspoon mustard
>  1  garlic clove, minced
>  Pinch of salt
>  2  teaspoons dried oregano
>  1  tablespoon Worcestershire sauce
>  3  tablespoons ketchup

1. Preheat the oven to 350°F.

2. Cut up the bread into small pieces.

3. In a large bowl, mix together all the ingredients except the ketchup.

4. Place this mix into a nonstick loaf pan.

5. Pour the ketchup on top of the meat.

6. Bake for 60 minutes.

7. Drain the grease. Let the meat loaf cool before serving.

# GOTTA HAVE HEART

Y ou might not like the sound of it, but cooked organ meat is music to a dog's stomach. Here's a recipe that costs pennies to make but will seem priceless to your dog.

2 beef hearts
1 cup white rice
¼ cup bread crumbs
2 garlic cloves, minced
2 tablespoons sunflower oil
1 cup water
½ cup finely grated carrots
½ cup finely grated turnips

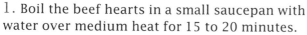

1. Boil the beef hearts in a small saucepan with water over medium heat for 15 to 20 minutes.

2. Steam the rice per package directions.

3. Chop the beef hearts into small pieces.

4. In a large bowl, blend the beef hearts, rice, bread crumbs, garlic, oil, water, carrots, and turnips thoroughly using a wooden spoon.

5. Allow to cool before serving. Store leftovers in the refrigerator.

# LEFTOVER HEAVEN

Your dog will think he's in heaven on earth when you serve up this hearty dish loaded with vegetables, protein, and a dash of vitamin C.

1 pound beef kidneys
2 garlic cloves, minced
1 cup water
1 cup diced carrots
1 cup diced zucchini
6 cups white rice
6 cups quick-cooking oats, uncooked
1 tablespoon safflower oil
1 tablespoon flaxseed oil
1 1,000-mg vitamin C supplement, crushed

1. Combine the beef kidneys and the garlic with the water in a large pot. Simmer over medium heat until the beef is cooked through. Add more water as necessary to maintain about one cup of water in the pot.

2. Steam the carrots and zucchini with a little water in the microwave oven on high for 3 minutes.

3. Steam the rice as per package directions.

4. Add the oats, cooked rice, carrots, zucchini, safflower oil, flaxseed oil, and vitamin C supplement to the pan containing the beef kidneys and garlic.

5. Remove from heat and stir thoroughly with a large spoon.

6. Allow to cool before serving. Store leftovers in a container in the refrigerator.

# PORK AND RICE STIR-FRY

In the mood for some Asian food tonight? Bring out the wok and prepare this stir-fry that both you and your dog can enjoy.

> 2 eggs, whisked
> 2 tablespoons olive oil, divided
> ¼ cup peas
> ¼ cup green beans
> 1 tablespoon fresh or 1 teaspoon dried parsley
> ½ cup chicken broth
> ½ pound roasted pork, thinly sliced
> 2 teaspoons soy sauce (low-sodium)
> 4 cups cooked rice

1. In a nonstick skillet, cook the eggs and one tablespoon of the oil over medium heat for a few minutes. Do not stir.

2. Place the eggs on a plate and cut into little pieces.

3. Heat the remaining oil in the skillet and stir-fry the peas, green beans, and parsley for a few minutes over medium heat.

4. Add the chicken broth, pork, and soy sauce and cook for 3 minutes.

5. Add the cooked rice and the egg to the skillet and cook for 3 minutes, stirring regularly.

6. Cool before serving. Store unused portions in a container in the refrigerator.

# FISH AND FOWL

**ats aren't the only critters** that crave a catch from the sea. Dogs also drool for the chance to reel in a tasty piece of cod. And your dog will certainly cry "Foul!" if you deny him an occasional home-cooked turkey or chicken dinner. Fish and fowl meals are among the best ways to show your dog how much you care for him. Both are loaded with healthy goodness but are low in calories and fat.

For years, fish has been touted as "brain power" food. Why not find out for yourself? Schedule your dog's training sessions after supper and see if he catches on to your "Sit," "Fetch," and "Stay" cues quickly. You may have a four-legged Einstein!

# FiDO'S FiSH DiSH

The next time you're at the supermarket, head for the fish counter and order a pound of this inexpensive fish for Fido.

    1   pound boneless cod fish
    ½   cup milk
    ½   cup water
    1   cup white rice
    ½   cup diced green peppers
    2   tablespoons vegetable oil
    3   hard-boiled eggs, mashed
    1   carrot, grated
    1   tablespoon fresh or 1 teaspoon dried parsley

1. Combine the fish, milk, and water in a pan over medium-low heat and simmer for 20 minutes.

2. Steam the rice per package directions.

3. Add the green peppers, oil, eggs, carrot, and parsley to the fish. Simmer for 5 minutes.

4. Serve this meal as a scoop of rice topped with ½ cup of the fish mix.

5. Store the leftovers in the refrigerator.

# GOTTA HAVE SOLE

Here's a simple, lip-smackin' recipe to satiate your fish-loving canine.

- ½  pound fillet of sole, deboned
- 2  tablespoons chopped fresh or 2 teaspoons dried parsley
- 1  tablespoon chopped fresh or 1 teaspoon dried cilantro
- 1  teaspoon salt
- 1  teaspoon pepper
- ⅔  cup white rice
- 1  tablespoon margarine
- 1  tablespoon white flour
- ½  cup milk
- ⅓  cup grated cheddar cheese

1. Preheat the oven to 450°F.

2. Spray a baking pan with nonstick cooking spray. Place the sole fillets in the pan.

3. Sprinkle the parsley, cilantro, salt, and pepper over the sole.

4. Add just enough water to cover the bottom of the pan.

5. Bake for 10 to 12 minutes.

6. Cook the rice per package directions.

7. In a larger pan, melt the margarine. Stir in the flour, and bring to a boil. Reduce to low heat.

8. Add the milk and stir until the mix thickens. Add the cheese and stir until melted.

9. In a large serving bowl, mix all the ingredients. Cool and serve.

10. Store unused portion in an airtight container inside the refrigerator.

# BARK-VA-LOUS DISH

Here's a melody of tastes that will have your dog singing.

- ½ pound ground chicken
- 1½ tablespoons vegetable oil, divided
- 2 garlic cloves, crushed
- 4 cups white rice
- 1 cup peeled and sliced sweet potato
- 1 cup diced green beans
- 1 carrot, diced

1. Brown the ground chicken in a pan with 1 tablespoon oil and the garlic. Drain.

2. Steam the rice per package instructions.

3. Sauté the sweet potato, green beans, and carrot with ½ tablespoon oil.

4. Combine all the ingredients and mix thoroughly.

5. Serve when cooled.

## SERVING STRATEGIES

Introducing your dog to the world of wonderful homemade meals is great, but it needs to be done carefully. Dogs are creatures of habit, and a radical change in their diet could cause upset, both behaviorally and physically. So when you try something different, you should make certain you are serving the right kinds of food in the right amounts and in the right way.

### Switch Slowly

If you're switching from one type of dog food to another, do so gradually or your dog may develop diarrhea or another digestive ailment. Start with just a small amount of the new food mixed into your dog's regular food. Increase that portion gradually, reducing the amount of regular food proportionately over 10 to 14 days to give your dog's digestive system ample time to adjust to the new cuisine.

### One Size Doesn't Fit All

How much should you feed your dog? That depends on your dog's age, level of activity, physical size, body metabolism, and physical health. A small dog, for example, generally needs only one cup of chow, but a giant breed may need three cups to meet his nutritional needs. The amount of food can also vary depending on a dog's situation. Pregnant or nursing females need more food than spayed females, and competitive agility dogs need more food than lap loungers. Consult with your veterinarian to determine a basic feeding guideline for your dog.

### Measure It Out

You may like to be creative and add a pinch of this or that to your homemade chili, but when it comes to feeding your dog, you need to bring out the measuring cups. Take the guesswork out of portion sizes by leveling off each scoop of food before pouring it into your dog's bowl. This provides you with a baseline. If your dog gains weight, you know to trim back on the size of each serving.

### Serve and Stroll

Many of us enjoy an evening stroll after dinner to help us burn up a bit of the meal's fat. An evening walk after a bowl full of chow seems to benefit our dogs, too. A recent study by the Division of Nutritional Sciences at Cornell University in Ithaca, New York, discovered that dogs that exercise after eating raise their body's rate of metabolism and burn more calories than dogs that lie down for a post-meal snooze. Veterinarians recommend mild to moderate exercise for a dog after feeding so that you don't cause him to have digestive upset.

# PAWSITIVELY PLEASING PASTA

On a chilly day, you can warm up your kitchen and your dog's heart with this tasty noodle dish.

| | |
|---|---|
| 2 | teaspoons olive oil |
| 1 | cup water |
| 2 | cups pasta noodles |
| 1 | cup chopped broccoli |
| 1 | cup chopped carrots |
| 1 | cup chopped cauliflower |
| 1½ | pounds ground turkey |
| ½ | teaspoon basil |
| ½ | teaspoon oregano |
| ½ | teaspoon garlic powder |
| ½ | teaspoon black pepper |
| 1 | 8-ounce can tomato sauce |
| ½ | cup chopped mushrooms |
| ¼ | cup black olives |

1. In a large pot, bring the oil and water to a boil. Add the pasta noodles.

2. In a separate pan, steam the broccoli, carrots, and cauliflower.

3. Brown the ground turkey in a skillet, with the basil, oregano, garlic powder, and black pepper. Add the tomato sauce, mushrooms, and black olives.

4. Drain the noodles. Pour the meat mix and steamed vegetables into the noodle pot. Mix with a wooden spoon.

5. Serve when cool. Store any leftovers in the refrigerator.

# SIT, STAY FOR TURKEY

Turkey is a healthy, low-fat meat to serve your dog. This turkey recipe is filled with vitamin- and mineral-rich supplements that support physical and emotional well-being.

2 cups water
1 cup uncooked rolled oats
3 eggs baked in the oven for
   10 minutes at 350°F
1 teaspoon calcium powder
1 teaspoon magnesium powder
1 teaspoon bonemeal powder
½ cup cottage cheese
1 cup grated carrots
½ cup ground turkey
1 teaspoon brewer's yeast (optional)

1. In a medium sized pot, bring the water to a boil.

2. Add the oats, cover, reduce heat to medium, and cook for 3 minutes.

3. Turn off the heat and let the pan stand for another 10 minutes, then add the rest of the ingredients.

4. Spoon the mixture into your dog's bowl when it is cool. As an added treat, sprinkle a teaspoon of brewer's yeast on top.

# TAIL-WAGGING TURKEY PIZZA

This recipe is one you can definitely enjoy with your dog on a Friday night — try not to fight too much over that last piece.

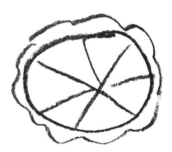

　¼　cup turkey broth
　　Premade pizza dough
　1　cup diced cooked turkey
　½　cup finely chopped spinach
　½　teaspoon garlic powder
　1　cup grated mozzarella cheese
　¼　cup sesame seeds

1. Preheat the oven to 375°F.

2. Pour the turkey broth over the pizza dough.

3. Sprinkle the turkey, spinach, garlic powder, cheese, and sesame seeds on top.

4. Place on a greased pizza sheet and bake for 12 to 15 minutes.

5. Enjoy your slice while it is warm, but let the slice for your dog cool before serving.

# YOUR EVOLVING DOG

As your dog ages from a puppy to a senior canine, his nutritional needs also evolve, and his diet should be tailored to best support each life stage. Food selection should be based on a dog's age, breed, activity level, and health condition. Young, growing puppies require a higher concentration of nutrients than dogs in their prime. Adult dogs need additional protein, while senior, less active dogs will burn off fewer calories than they did in their Frisbee-chasing youth.

# CHOWHOUND CHICKEN SOUP

Fortify your dog on a chilly day with this warm-to-the-soul soup.

- 2 chicken breasts or thighs
- 5 cups water
- 2 large carrots, peeled and diced
- 1 celery stalk, chopped
- 2 potatoes, peeled and cubed
- 2 cups rice, uncooked

1. Combine the chicken, water, carrots, celery, and potatoes in a large pot.

2. Cover and simmer over low heat for 2 hours, stirring occasionally.

3. Add the rice and continuing simmering over low heat for 30 to 35 minutes, or until most of the liquid has been absorbed.

4. Remove from the stovetop and let the soup cool.

5. Pull the meat off the chicken bones. Put the meat back in the soup and toss the bones in the trash.

6. Stir the soup before serving.

7. Store leftovers in the refrigerator.

# VEGETARIAN MEALS

**n this day and age** of health-conscious consumers, more and more humans are eating less and less meat, and many have decided to forgo meat entirely, making the leap to vegetarianism. Dogs, of course, are not naturally vegetarians. They are omnivores, designed to thrive on both meat and plants.

Completely vegetarian diets are not generally recommended for dogs. However, an occasional vegetarian meal can be quite healthful. Most vegetables are rich in the antioxidants, vitamins, and minerals that your dog's body craves, and they make a welcome treat for your dog. Some of the recipes in this chapter also feature tofu, a terrific protein source often touted by health care professionals for its nutritional benefits.

Whenever possible, select vegetables that were organically grown. Pesticides and herbicides leave only a small residue on vegetables, but many health care experts believe that they can build up in the system over time, possibly leading to health problems. If organic vegetables are not available, be sure to carefully wash the produce you do buy.

# MOLLIE'S MARVELOUS VEGGIE CASSEROLE

Mollie, a 12-year-old Cocker Spaniel that proudly sports pink ribbons on her blond ears, possesses pup-like energy. She's also one lucky dog. Her owner, Barbara Lee of Lake San Marcos, California, a longtime vegetarian, cooks most of Mollie's meals, using mostly organically grown ingredients. Mollie especially barks approval for this dish.

1 cup chopped cauliflower
1 cup chopped broccoli
1 cup chopped carrots
1 cup chopped green beans
1 clove garlic, crushed
1 tablespoon olive oil
1 teaspoon salt
½ teaspoon black pepper
2 tablespoons grated Parmesan cheese

1. Steam the vegetables in a large pan over medium heat.

2. Add the garlic, olive oil, salt, and black pepper. Stir well. Cover the pot, reduce the heat to low, and simmer for 10 minutes.

3. Pour into a large serving container and drain off excess water. Sprinkle with the cheese.

4. Allow to cool before serving.

# DOGGY VITTLES

Treat your vegetable-loving dog to this fortifying dish.

>  1  cup cooked rice
> ⅔ cup grated cheese
> ½ cup finely chopped carrots
> ½ cup finely chopped zucchini
> ⅓ cup applesauce
>  1  egg, beaten
>  1  tablespoon brewer's yeast

1. Preheat the oven to 350˚F.

2. Combine all the ingredients in a large bowl. Blend thoroughly.

3. Pour the mix into a casserole dish.

4. Bake for 12 to 15 minutes.

5. Cool and serve. Store leftovers in the refrigerator.

# NO-MEAT STEW

♡ ♡ ♡ ♡ ♡

What? No meat? No problem. Your dog will lap up this hearty stew and beg for seconds!

- 3 tablespoons olive oil
- 2 garlic cloves, crushed
- 1 potato, peeled and diced
- 1 green pepper, diced
- 1 zucchini, sliced
- 1 yellow squash, sliced
- 1 eggplant, peeled and diced
- 1 24-ounce can of tomatoes, chopped (save the juice)
- 1 teaspoon basil
- 1 teaspoon sugar
- ½ teaspoon salt
- ½ teaspoon pepper

1. In a saucepan, heat the olive oil. Add the garlic and sauté for 2 minutes.

2. Add the vegetables, tomatoes with juice, basil, sugar, and seasonings.

3. Bring to a boil, then reduce the heat to low and let simmer, covered, for 30 to 40 minutes.

4. Let cool before serving.

# PAWS-UP POTATO CASSEROLE

♡♡♡♡♡

Here's a sensational spud dish for your bud.

    3  medium potatoes, sliced thin
    ½  cup canned corn
    ½  cup cottage cheese
    1  carrot, grated
    ¼  cup milk
    1  tablespoon brewer's yeast
    ¼  cup grated cheddar cheese

1. Preheat the oven to 350°F.

2. Layer the bottom of a medium-sized casserole dish with the sliced potatoes.

3. Arrange the corn, cottage cheese, and carrot in layers on top of the potatoes.

4. Slowly pour the milk over the layered vegetables.

5. Top the dish by sprinkling on the yeast and the cheese.

6. Bake for 15 to 20 minutes, or until the cheese melts and turns a golden brown.

7. Serve cool.

# LiP-SMACKiNG GREEN BEANS

This glorious green dish is perfect for St. Patrick's Day —
or any day, for that matter.

1 15-ounce can cream of mushroom
soup
½ cup skim milk
1 tablespoon Worcestershire sauce
1 pound green beans, cooked and sliced
½ cup grated cheddar cheese

1. Preheat the oven to 350°F.

2. In a medium bowl, blend the soup, milk,
and Worcestershire sauce.

3. Place the green beans on the bottom of a casserole dish. Pour the soup
mixture over them.

4. Cover with aluminum foil and bake in the oven for 25 to 30 minutes.

5. Remove the cover and sprinkle the cheese on top.

6. Return to the oven and bake for 5 minutes more, or until the cheese
has melted.

7. Cool before serving.

# TEMPTING TOFU

ofu is the chameleon of all foods — it tastes like whatever it is cooked with. Even better, it's loaded with soy, a good source of protein.

> 4 ounces tofu, in small cubes
> 3 tablespoons sunflower oil, divided
> 2 cups kidney beans
> 2 cups whole grain rice
> A vitamin-mineral daily supplement
>    for dogs, crushed

1. Fry the tofu with 1 tablespoon oil in a pan on the stovetop. Add the kidney beans and cook over low heat for 10 to 15 minutes.

2. Steam the rice per package directions.

3. In a large bowl, blend the tofu–bean mixture with the rice, remaining oil, and vitamin-mineral supplement.

4. Let cool before serving.

## THE FACTS ON FIBER

iber, in the right amounts, can be a dog's best friend. It lets your dog feel full on fewer calories. Too little fiber in your dog's diet can lead to diarrhea. Too much can cause constipation and dehydration. Work with your veterinarian to find a good balance.

Good fiber sources include apple and tomato pomace, citrus pulp, oat bran, peanut hulls, rice bran, soybean hulls, and wheat.

# MAC ATTACK
✳ ✳ ✳ ✳

Think your kids are the only ones that crave macaroni? Just try out this recipe on your dog and watch him go bow-WOW!

>     1 12-ounce box elbow macaroni
>     2 tablespoons margarine
>     2 tablespoons whole wheat flour
>     1 cup milk
>     8 ounces jack cheese, grated

1. Cook the macaroni per package directions. Drain and set aside.

2. Melt the margarine in a large skillet over low heat. Stir in the flour. Once the flour forms a paste, add the milk and continue to stir for 5 minutes, or until the mixture thickens.

3. Add the cheese and let it melt. Remove the skillet from the stove.

4. Pour the sauce over the hot macaroni and stir.

5. Cool before serving. Store unused portions in a container in the refrigerator.

# SÍ, SÍ TORTILLAS

✳ ✳ ✳ ✳

Become your dog's best amigo — or amiga — by preparing these sweet-tasting tortillas.

    1  tablespoon vegetable oil
    4  large corn tortillas
    ⅓  cup brown sugar
    1  teaspoon cinnamon

1. In a large skillet, heat the vegetable oil over medium heat.

2. Lightly brown the tortillas on both sides, cooking one at a time. Add more oil as needed to keep the bottom of the skillet coated.

3. Place the tortillas on paper towels to absorb excess grease.

4. Sprinkle the tortillas with the brown sugar and cinnamon.

5. Cut the tortillas into bite-size pieces and serve when cooled.

## HEALTHY HERBS FOR DOGS

Using herbs to improve human health and well-being is not a recent fad; it goes back to the earliest origins of human medicine. But for creatures like your dog, it goes back much farther than that. Animals have always instinctively sought out the plants that their bodies need to cure a variety of conditions. Have you ever seen your pup chew grass? Somehow he just knows that this will help settle an upset stomach. With the greater knowledge we have today of many herbs and their effects, it is easy to discover some that will give you a healthier, happier dog.

### Start Out Slowly and Safely

Before treating your dog with herbs, particularly to solve a physical condition or illness, be sure to check with your veterinarian. Always consult a vet before giving any herb to a pregnant or nursing dog or a puppy. The safest way to administer herbs is to start with a low dosage, observe the effects for a month or so, and adjust the amount accordingly. The right amount of herbs will be whatever is just enough to have the desired effect.

### Different Herbs for Different Results

With a little research and some consultation with a holistic veterinarian or an herbalist, you can find a wide range of herbs to give to your dog. Here are a few common herbs and the effects they may have.

**Calendula** is used externally to treat wounds and skin irritations.
**Chamomile** alleviates anxiety, insomnia, and indigestion.
**Echinacea** stimulates and strengthens the immune system.
**Peppermint** soothes gas, indigestion, and colic.
**Slippery elm** settles nervous stomachs and eases diarrhea.

### A Little Sprinkle on Top

The easiest way to serve your dog herbs is to chop them fine and sprinkle them on top of his meals, whether it's one of homemade or commercial dog food. Proper amounts will range from a small pinch for a small dog to several teaspoons for a 100-pounder. You could also mix herbs into one of the recipes in this book. Fresh herbs are generally more potent than dried herbs and usually keep their flavor better when sprinkled, though dried herbs are easier to keep on hand year-round.

### Herbal Teatime

A soothing cup of herbal tea always makes you feel better, doesn't it? Well, it can do the same for your dog. Pour 1 cup of boiling water over 1 to 2 teaspoons dried herbs or 2 to 4 tablespoons fresh herbs. Cover, let steep for 10 to 15 minutes, strain well, and let cool. You can then pour the herbal mixture over your dog's food. If your dog prefers his food unadulterated, you can instead administer an herbal tea by squirting it into his mouth, along his lower back teeth, with a plastic syringe.

# POOCH PANCAKES

Begin your dog's day with this hearty breakfast.

 2  white potatoes
 2  tablespoons vegetable oil, divided
 1  egg
 ¼  cup flour
 Pinch of salt
 Pinch of black pepper
 2  cups pancake mix
 1  cup water
 ⅓  cup grated cheddar cheese

1. Peel and grate the potatoes.

2. Coat the bottom of a large skillet with 1 tablespoon of the vegetable oil, and warm over medium heat.

3. Place the potatoes in the skillet and sauté, stirring frequently, for 3 to 5 minutes.

4. Add the egg, flour, salt, and pepper.

5. Mix potato and egg mixture with the pancake mix and water in a medium-sized bowl. Stir in cheese.

6. Heat the remaining oil in a separate skillet.

7. Pour ¼ cup of the pancake mixture into the hot oil. Fry on both sides until golden brown.

8. Place the pancake on a paper towel to absorb excess oil, and repeat steps 7 and 8 to make more pancakes.

9. Cool before serving.

# MAGGIE SAYS YUM TO YAMS

**M**aggie, a German Shepherd mix who once traveled around Florida to research pet-friendly destinations for a travel guidebook *(The Florida Dog Lover's Companion),* became a finicky eater at age 15 — much to the surprise of her owners, Robert McClure and Sally Deneen of Seattle, Washington, who previously never met a better eater.

They tried heating her high-quality commercial canned dog food, adding bouillon for extra flavor, and even tossing in bits of cooked liver and pork, but she ate it half-heartedly.

Concerned, they consulted Maggie's acupuncturist, Craig Thompson of Lynnwood, Washington. He said that not only would homemade food be better for old Maggie, but she'd gobble it up, too. He suggested this formula: two parts cooked chicken, liver, or pork to one part steamed yams and one part cooked brown rice. Maggie now wolfs down her food, easily finishing in less than a minute. Says Maggie: Yum!

# SPINACH SURPRISE

Popeye would be proud to know your dog devours this iron-rich vegetable.

   1  10-ounce package frozen
      chopped spinach, thawed
   4  garlic cloves, minced
   2  teaspoons peanut oil
  ⅓  cup chicken broth

1. Remove the spinach from the box and squeeze out the excess water.

2. In a large skillet, sauté the garlic in the oil over medium heat for 3 to 5 minutes.

3. Add the spinach and stir well.

4. Slowly pour in the chicken broth and cover the skillet. Simmer for 2 minutes.

5. Remove from heat and serve when cooled.

# SPECIAL OCCASION MEALS

**id your dog just have a birthday?** Did he just graduate — with honors — from puppy kindergarten class, or wow the crowd by garnering blue ribbons at the local agility event? It's time to celebrate these feats, and what better way than with some of these fantastic feasts!

Never overlook the opportunity to share a joyful occasion with your dog. He may not understand the words, "You were the valedictorian of your dog obedience class," but he will certainly read your body language and your upbeat voice to know something great just happened.

Save these recipes for special occasions so that your dog will recognize their supreme importance. You will forever reign as the champion of the kitchen in his mind and heart.

# MUNCHY PUP-CAKES

Coco, a black Poodle, looks forward to her birthday each year. That's because her owner, Susan Baker of Atlantis, Florida, loves to usher in the special day with this cupcake recipe.

"Coco is very good about eating her commercial dog food, but her whole body starts wiggling with delight when I pull these cupcakes out of the oven," says Baker.

You, too, can celebrate your dog's big day. Invite a few of his four-legged friends over to help him gulp down these goodies.

> 3 cups water
> 2 carrots, shredded
> 1 egg
> ½ teaspoon vanilla
> 2 tablespoons honey
> 2 ripe bananas, mashed
> 4 cups whole wheat flour
> 1 teaspoon baking powder
> 1 teaspoon nutmeg
> 1 teaspoon cinnamon

1. Preheat the oven to 350°F.

2. In a large mixing bowl, blend the water, carrots, egg, vanilla, and honey. Add the mashed bananas.

3. In a separate bowl, mix the flour, baking powder, nutmeg, and cinnamon.

4. Pour the flour mixture into the carrot mixture and mix thoroughly.

5. Spray a 12-cupcake pan with nonstick spray.

6. Fill each cup about three-quarters full.

7. Bake for 50 to 60 minutes.

8. Cool before serving.

oh please

## HALT THOSE BEGGIN' EYES

Dogs are masters at projecting that pitiful look of starvation — even if their bellies are touching the floor. If you have trouble saying no to those begging eyes, try feeding your dog when your family eats breakfast or dinner — but feed him in a different room, out of your sight. And, the next time your dog comes begging, give him hugs instead. They're calorie free!

# FIDO THANKSGIVING FEAST

Allow your dog to participate in the Thanksgiving festivities with this special dish.

> 1 teaspoon olive oil
> ½ cup mashed potatoes
> 1 egg
> ½ cup diced cooked turkey meat
> ½ cup chopped broccoli
> ⅓ cup grated cheddar cheese

1. Warm the olive oil in a medium-sized pan over medium heat.

2. In a small bowl, whisk together the potatoes and egg.

3. Pour the potato and egg mix into the pan. Add the turkey and broccoli.

4. Cover the pan, reduce heat to low, and simmer until the egg is cooked.

5. Top with the grated cheese and let it cook for a few minutes longer to allow the cheese to melt.

6. Let cool before serving.

# BEANS AND BACON STIR-FRY

**B**eans and bacon. Your first reaction may be "ugh," but your dog will bark out, "Bring on the B&B!" Use this dish to celebrate very special occasions — birthdays, the successful end of housebreaking, a return home from a stay at the vet, and so on.

> 3 strips bacon
> 1 16-ounce can kidney beans
> 3 carrots, peeled and diced
> 3 garlic cloves, minced
> 3 celery stalks, diced
> 3 tablespoons chopped fresh or
>   3 teaspoons dried parsley
> 1 teaspoon apple vinegar
> Pinch of black pepper

1. Cook the bacon strips in a large skillet. Do not drain the grease. Break up the bacon into little pieces.

2. Warm the kidney beans in a separate pan over medium heat for 5 minutes. Stir often.

3. Add the carrots, garlic, and celery to the skillet with the bacon. Cook over medium heat for a few minutes, stirring occasionally.

4. Add the beans, parsley, apple vinegar, and pepper to the mix.

5. Cool before serving.

## WEIGHTY MATTERS

Your pampered pooch might be getting a few too many treats and not quite enough exercise. These tips can help you to adjust his diet and keep him fit and trim.

### Rely on the Rib Test

Is your dog at his ideal weight? Ralston Purina developed this fit and trim rib test:

First, place your thumbs on your dog's backbone and spread your hands across his rib cage. You should be able to feel your dog's ribs.

Look at your dog's profile while he is standing. He should have a clearly defined abdomen slightly tucked up behind his rib cage.

Stand over your standing dog. Most dogs have an hourglass shape, and you should be able to see his waist.

### Watch Out for Sneaky Snacks

Snacks quickly add up in calories and are often overlooked factors behind your dog's walk turning into a waddle. Best advice: Factor in your dog's treats with his regular meals when you count calories. Limit your dog's treats to no more than 10 percent of his total daily food portions.

### Beef Up on the Veggies

One healthy weight-loss strategy calls
for adding more steamed vegetables to
your dog's chow and reducing amounts
of fatty meats. The vegetables are low
in calories but help satisfy your dog's
appetite so that he leaves the bowl
feeling full.

### Lay Off the Sauce — and the Oil

One teaspoon of vegetable oil equals about
50 calories. For a small dog that needs only 300
calories a day to maintain its weight, that one teaspoon equals
one-sixth of its total calories. Go easy on the sauces and oils in
food preparation.

### Boil, Not Fry

Minimize the amount of unhealthy fat in your dog's dinner by
boiling, broiling, baking, or steaming meats and fish — don't ever
fry foods. Avoid cooking with lard or coconut oil (both are loaded
with saturated fats).

### Try Smarter Treats

If you have trouble resisting your dog's begging, switch to
these healthy treats, which are low in calories and high in nutritional value:

- Air-popped popcorn
- Apple slices
- Broccoli
- Carrots

# "GO FETCH" STEW

Your dog may never tire of retrieving that beloved tennis ball — at least not before you do — and he won't get tired of eating this tasty dish, either.

   3  tablespoons vegetable oil
   3  pounds lamb (remove the fat and cut into 1-inch cubes)
   1  apple, peeled, cored, and diced
   1  teaspoon paprika
   1  teaspoon allspice
   1  cinnamon stick
  ½  teaspoon ground cinnamon
   1  6-ounce can tomato paste
1½  cups water
  ¼  cup apple vinegar

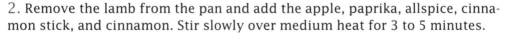

1. In a large nonstick skillet, heat the oil over medium heat. Add the lamb and brown on all sides.

2. Remove the lamb from the pan and add the apple, paprika, allspice, cinnamon stick, and cinnamon. Stir slowly over medium heat for 3 to 5 minutes.

3. Put the browned lamb back into the pan and add the tomato paste and water. Bring to a simmer.

4. Reduce to low heat, cover the pan and let the ingredients simmer for 1 hour. Then add the apple vinegar and simmer for 15 minutes longer.

5. Cool before serving.

# SERVING DISHES

Select food and water bowls that are easy to clean and resistant to chewing or breaking. If you have a dog with long ears and a long nose, select a food bowl with high sides so that his ears will not get caught inside the bowl and get covered with food. If you have more than one dog, give each his own food bowl.

# BIRTHDAY BREAKFAST BONANZA

Here's a speedy dish that adds a festive tone to your dog's Big Day. You might even want to make a portion for yourself to share in the celebration.

> 1 tablespoon margarine
> 3 eggs
> 2 ham slices, diced
> 2 cheddar cheese slices

1. Heat the margarine in a nonstick skillet over medium heat.

2. Add the eggs and scramble until they are fluffy.

3. Add the ham and cheese slices and stir until well mixed.

4. Remove from heat and cool before serving.

# SPECIAL DIETS

Often, the way to a dog's heart — and good health — is through his stomach. What you feed your dog is very important, especially if he is a growing puppy or a senior dog or has a medical condition. In this section, you'll find a heaping sampling of some healing homemade meals that cater to many conditions. But before you head off to the supermarket or don your apron, book an appointment with your veterinarian. Work together on devising meal plans that complement your dog's commercial dry food and that best meet your dog's specific needs.

Many of the recipes here are provided courtesy of Lowell Ackerman, D.V.M., of Boston, Massachusetts, an expert on canine nutrition and a pretty good cook, too!

# PUPPY GROWTH DIET

Help your puppy grow big and strong by occasionally treating him to this nutritious meal.

        3 ounces ground beef
        1 cup rice
        3 ounces small-curd cottage cheese
        1 hard-boiled egg, mashed
        1 carrot, diced
        Contents of a 500-mg psyllium husk capsule
        1 teaspoon corn oil
        1 1,000-mg calcium supplement, crushed

1. Cook the ground beef in a pan over medium heat. Drain excess grease.

2. Steam the rice per package directions.

3. Mix the ground beef and rice in a bowl. Then add the cottage cheese, egg, carrot, and psyllium husks.

4. Add the oil and let it soak in. Add the calcium.

5. Cool before serving.

## WATER-LOGGED DOG

In newborn puppies, water makes up about 85 percent of body weight. In adult dogs, water constitutes about 50 percent of body weight.

# MEAL FOR ACTIVE DOGS

Does your dog leap at the chance to compete in agility events? Or is he always rarin' to go when you hold up the leash? Here's a great meal for a high-energy dog.

>     4 ounces lean ground beef
>     2 cups white rice
>     1 large carrot, puréed in a blender
>   Contents of a 500-mg psyllium husk capsule
>   1½ teaspoons sunflower oil
>     3 slices whole wheat bread
>     1 750-mg calcium supplement, crushed

1. Cook the ground beef over medium heat. Drain excess grease.

2. Steam the rice per package directions.

3. Mix the ground beef with the rice. Add the carrot, psyllium husks, and oil and let soak for 5 minutes.

4. Cut up the bread slices and stir into the mix.

5. Add the calcium supplement before serving.

# MEAL FOR SENIOR DOGS

Show a little tenderness for your gray-muzzled friend by treating her to this dish.

> 6 ounces skinless chicken breast
> 1½ cup white rice
> 1 sweet potato
> 2 tablespoons corn oil
> 1 1,000-mg calcium supplement, crushed
> Liquid contents of a 100 IU vitamin E capsule

1. Broil the chicken breast until thoroughly cooked.

2. Steam the rice per package directions.

3. Microwave the sweet potato until a fork slides easily in and out. Peel and mash the potato.

4. Mix the chicken with the sweet potato and then stir in the rice.

5. Add the oil, calcium, and vitamin E and stir again.

6. Cool before serving.

## AGING DOGS NEED PROTEIN

As dogs age, they need extra protein to preserve muscle mass. Protein supplies the building blocks of muscles and fortifies the immune system. But also keep in mind that dogs in their golden years burn one-half or even one-quarter as many calories as young dogs, so check with your veterinarian on how much to scale back on your dog's daily serving amounts.

# SUPPLEMENT ALERT

Supplements should be added to your dog's diet
only to:
- Compensate for a known nutrient deficiency
  (as determined by a blood test).
- Trigger food intake during times when a dog is
  nursing a litter or performing hard work.
- Optimize the amount of a certain nutrient to
  prevent disease or treat a chronic condition.

Be careful. When it comes to supplements, the adage
"More is better" does not apply. If you give your dog
too much calcium, you can cause harm to joints and
bones. Too much copper or zinc can be toxic to your
dog. Always work with your veterinarian in determining which supplements and how much should be
given to your dog to meet its special needs.

# DOGGIE DIET FOR INACTIVE CANINES

Does it seem as though your laid-back dog has become a fixture on your sofa? Does he yawn more than yap? Here's a low-calorie meal that will rev up his taste buds. If your dog begs for snacks between meals, offer popped popcorn (no butter or salt) and plain lettuce.

3 ounces skinless chicken breast
1 sweet potato
1 large carrot
1 teaspoon sunflower oil
Contents of 2 500-mg psyllium husk capsules
1 750-mg calcium supplement

1. Broil the chicken breast until thoroughly cooked.

2. Steam the sweet potato in the microwave until a fork slides easily in and out. Peel and mash the potato.

3. Cut the chicken into small pieces and mix them with the mashed sweet potato in a bowl.

4. Chop the carrot into small pieces.

5. Add the carrot, oil, psyllium husks, and calcium supplement to the mix and stir well. Serve cool.

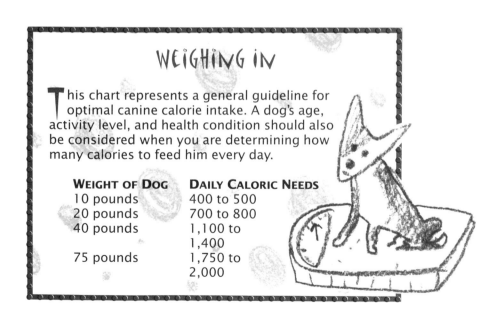

## WEIGHING IN

This chart represents a general guideline for optimal canine calorie intake. A dog's age, activity level, and health condition should also be considered when you are determining how many calories to feed him every day.

| WEIGHT OF DOG | DAILY CALORIC NEEDS |
|---------------|---------------------|
| 10 pounds | 400 to 500 |
| 20 pounds | 700 to 800 |
| 40 pounds | 1,100 to 1,400 |
| 75 pounds | 1,750 to 2,000 |

# HYPOALLERGENIC DIET

Ah-choo! For dogs sensitive to certain foods, Dr. Ackerman offers this safe but savory meal.

4 ounces lamb
½ cup white rice
1 medium sweet potato
1 large carrot, chopped
1 teaspoon safflower oil
Contents of a 500-mg psyllium husk capsule
1 750-mg calcium supplement, crushed

1. Trim excess fat from the lamb meat and then broil until thoroughly cooked.

2. Steam the rice per package directions.

3. Microwave the sweet potato until a fork slides easily in and out. Peel and mash the potato.

4. In a large bowl, cut the cooked lamb into small pieces and mix with the cooked rice and mashed sweet potato.

5. Add the carrot, psyllium husks, and oil and allow to soak for 5 minutes.

6. Add the calcium supplement and serve.

## WHAT ARE SPECIAL-PURPOSE DIETS?

Pregnant or nursing dogs, fast-growing puppies, senior citizen canines, and arthritic dogs often have special nutritional requirements above and beyond those of a healthy dog in his prime. For example, pregnant or nursing females or working dogs often require higher-than-normal amounts of protein in their daily diets. Consult with your veterinarian or a member of the American College of Veterinary Nutrition to customize a diet that best meets your dog's special needs.

## ALLEVIATING ALLERGIES

*Before*

*Choo*

No, I don't mean dealing with your visiting Aunt Mary, who sneezes every time your pal Biggles comes within 30 feet. Here we're talking about allergies your dog may have to specific foods. These can be difficult to discover, but they are easy to deal with once you know which offending foods to avoid.

### What is a Food Allergy?

Sometimes a food allergy is confused with food intolerance, which results from an inability to digest a particular food (such as lactose intolerance). A food allergy is an abnormal immune response to a particular food or additive. Signs of a food allergy include itching and other skin problems or possibly gastronomical disturbances such as diarrhea.

Food allergies can occur in any dog at any age. They develop over time with repeated exposure to the same foods. Food intolerance can occur the first time a food is introduced. Another characteristic of a food allergy is its appearance year-round. Other allergies (such as flea allergy dermatitis) may be seasonal.

### Tracking Down Food Allergies

*After*

If you suspect your dog is allergic to a certain food, have your veterinarian give your dog a physical exam. Provide your veterinarian with a complete medical and dietary history of your dog. Then, the two of you can set up an elimination trial in which you isolate suspected foods — one at a time — and determine whether any is triggering an allergic reaction in your dog. It is a time-consuming process, so practice patience.

# GLOSSARY

**AMINO ACIDS.** These are the building blocks of protein. When a dog eats protein, his body breaks it down into amino acids, which are then absorbed by his body. The ten essential amino acids for dogs are arginine, histidine, isoleucine, leucine, lysine, methionine, phenylalanine, threonine, tryptophan, and valine.

**ANTIOXIDANTS.** These compounds protect cell membranes against harmful molecules known as free radicals. Free radicals can damage membranes and trigger heart disease, cancer, arthritis, and other degenerative diseases. Mixed tocopherols (compounds that promote antioxidant activity) are often added to commercial dog food to prevent rancidity and preserve freshness.

**CALORIE.** A unit by which energy is measured. Food energy is measured in kilocalories (1,000 calories equal 1 kilocalorie). One kilocalorie is the amount of energy needed to heat one kilogram of water one degree Celsius.

**CARBOHYDRATES.** Sugars, starches, and fibers comprise carbohydrates, the body's primary source of energy. Simple carbohydrates, called sugars, include honey, white table sugar, and natural sugars found in fruits, vegetables, and milk. Complex carbohydrates, called starches, are found in foods like cooked beans, oatmeal, pasta, potatoes, and rice.

**CARNIVORE.** An animal that eats only meat.

**CHONDROITIN SULFATES.** These long chains of sugar molecules act like magnets to attract fluid into the joint's cartilage matrix. With proper amounts of fluid, joints move more easily.

**DIETARY FAT.** This nutrient is a concentrated source of energy, improves the taste of foods, aids in digestion, and transports the fat-soluble vitamins A, D, E, and K throughout the body. Compared to carbohydrates and protein, fats contain about 2.5 times more energy per pound.

**FIBER.** This is a catch-all term for the tissue found in the seeds, leaves, and stems of plants. Fiber aids the passage of food through the digestive system and helps form firm stools. Dietary fiber also provides a feeling of fullness.

**FLAVORING AGENTS.** Ingredients added to foods to make them more palatable and appealing.

**FREE RADICALS.** Highly reactive and destructive molecules made inside the body. They contain one or more unpaired electrons and create chemical imbalances by stealing electrons from healthy molecules. Unchecked, free radicals can cause premature aging and contribute to chronic diseases.

**GLUCOSE.** A monosaccharide better known as blood sugar or dextrose.

**HERBIVORE.** An animal that eats only plants.

**IMMUNE SYSTEM.** The body's internal army that identifies and battles foreign invaders such as viruses and bacterium.

**LACTOSE INTOLERANCE.** A condition that results from the inability to digest lactose, a milk sugar, and causes bloating, gas, diarrhea, and other gastro-intestinal symptoms.

**METABOLISM.** The rate by which the body builds up and breaks down the chemicals it needs to live.

**MINERALS.** These inorganic elements are needed for normal body functions plus bone and tissue development. Major minerals include calcium, chloride, magnesium, phosphorus, potassium, sodium, and sulfur. Trace minerals consist of chromium, copper, fluoride, iodine, iron, manganese, molybdenum, selenium, and zinc.

**OMNIVORE.** An animal that eats meat and plants.

**ORGANIC.** This term refers to meats, grains, and fruits free of commercial fertilizers or pesticides as well as artificial colors, flavors, or preservatives.

**PROTEIN.** Protein repairs tissue, provides energy, ensures muscle growth, and aids the body's immune system. Growing puppies generally require more protein in their diets than older adult dogs. Non-meat sources of protein include soybean meal and tofu.

**VITAMINS.** Organic, essential nutrients required in small amounts by the body to promote and regulate various physiological processes. Water-soluble vitamins include vitamin C and the eight B vitamins (thiamine, riboflavin, niacin, $B_6$, $B_{12}$, folate, biotin, and pantothenic acid). Fat-soluble vitamins consist of vitamins A, D, E, and K.

**WATER.** Your dog's life depends on clean water. Water helps regulate body temperature, keeps the tissues lubricated, digests food, and flushes out toxins and waste matter. Provide fresh drinking water in a clean bowl for your dog every day.

# REFERENCES

## Books

*Canine Nutrition: What Every Owner, Breeder, and Trainer Should Know,* by Lowell Ackerman, D.V.M. (Alpine Publications, 1999).

*Dr. Pitcairn's Complete Guide to Natural Health for Dogs & Cats,* by Richard H. Pitcairn, D.V.M., Ph.D., and Susan Hubble Pitcairn (Rodale, 1995).

*The Dog: Its Behavior, Nutrition & Health,* by Linda P. Case (Iowa State University Press, 1999).

*50 Simple Ways To Pamper Your Dog,* by Arden Moore (Storey Books, 2000).

## Web Sites

PetDiets.com
*www.petdiets.com*
At this site, board-certified veterinary nutritionists will provide for a fee a personalized homemade diet formulation for your dog. All recipes are guaranteed to be nutritionally balanced and complete.

Ralston/Purina
*www.fitandtrim.com*
This pet-food company's site provides sound nutritional and fitness advice.

Hill's Pet Nutrition
*www.petfit.com*
The Pet Fit Challenge site offers on-target tips for keeping your dog in shape.

# INDEX

# METRIC CONVERSIONS AND U.S. EQUIVALENTS

Conversions between U.S. and metric measurements will be somewhat inexact, unless you have very precise measuring equipment. Be sure to convert the measurements for all of the ingredients in a recipe to maintain the same proportions as the original.

### GENERAL FORMULAS FOR METRIC CONVERSION

| | |
|---|---|
| Ounces to grams | multiply ounces by 28.35 |
| Pounds to grams | multiply pounds by 453.5 |
| Pounds to kilograms | multiply pounds by 0.45 |
| Cups to liters | multiply cups by 0.24 |
| Fahrenheit to Celsius | subtract 32 from Fahrenheit temperature, multiply by 5, then divide by 9 |

### APPROXIMATE METRIC EQUIVALENTS BY VOLUME

| U.S. | METRIC |
|---|---|
| 1 teaspoon | 5 milliliters |
| 1 tablespoon | 15 milliliters |
| ¼ cup | 60 milliliters |
| ½ cup | 120 milliliters |
| 1 cup | 230 milliliters |
| 2 cups | 460 milliliters |
| 4 cups (1 quart) | 0.95 liter |

# OTHER STOREY TITLES
# YOU WILL ENJOY

**50 Simple Ways to Pamper Your Dog,** by Arden Moore. Fun ideas for how to shower a pooch with love, affection, home-baked treats, and all the rewards that your loyal canine deserves. 144 pages. Paperback. ISBN 1-58017-310-1.

**Real Food for Cats: 50 Vet-Approved Recipes to Please the Feline Gastronome,** by Patti Delmonte. Vet-approved, wonderfully easy recipes to make for the finicky cat. Includes tips on cat care and health, plus delightful illustrations by Anne Davis. Also offers prescription diets for cats with special needs. 128 pages. Paperback. ISBN 1-58017-409-4.

**The Puppy Owner's Manual,** by Diana Delmar. In a fun question-and-answer format, Diana Delmar offers humane, commonsense solutions for chewing, barking, grooming, eating, house training, and other puppy problems. 192 pages. Paperback. ISBN 1-58017-401-9.

**The Kitten Owner's Manual,** by Arden Moore. Hundreds of practical tips on how to raise a happy, healthy, and well-adjusted cat, as well as answers to every kitten owner's most frequently asked questions. 192 pages. Paperback. ISBN 1-58017-387-X.

**Dr. Kidd's Guide to Herbal Dog Care,** by Randy Kidd, D.V.M., Ph.D. Readers learn how to use natural methods, such as herbal remedies and massage, to help maintain their dog's health. 208 pages. Paperback. ISBN 1-58017-189-3.

**The Guilt-Free Dog Owner's Guide: Caring for a Dog When You're Short on Time and Space,** by Diana Delmar. Easy-to-implement information removes the anxieties associated with selecting the right dog, housebreaking, exercise, manners, behavior problems, home hazards, travel, and dog health. 180 pages. Paperback. ISBN 0-88266-575-8.

**Your Puppy, Your Dog: A Kid's Guide to Raising a Happy, Healthy Dog,** by Pat Storer. Both parents and children can use this thorough guide to choosing, feeding, grooming, exercising, and training a puppy. 160 pages. Paperback. ISBN 0-88266-959-1.

*These books and other Storey books are available at your bookstore, farm store, garden center, or directly from Storey Books, 210 MASS MoCA Way, North Adams, MA 01247, or by calling 1-800-441-5700. Or visit our Web site at www.storey.com.*